Authentic Assessment

Concetta Doti Ryan, M.A.

Teacher Created Materials, Inc.

Illustrations by: Adam Doti

Made in U.S.A.
ISBN 1-55734-838-3

Order Number TCM 838

Table of Contents

Introduction

As our instructional practices and activities become more authentic, so must our assessment practices. Multiple choice tests do not give us accurate and reliable information regarding student's reading or writing abilities. Furthermore, with the renewed focus on hands-on activities in math, science, and social studies once again standardized tests fall short of being able to supply us with true information on student ability because they require acquisition, not application of knowledge. Authentic assessments such as portfolios, performance tasks, and miscue analysis can serve to better inform us regarding students' growth and progress. Also, because authentic assessment is ongoing and students are assessed throughout the course of study, teachers are in a better position to make necessary instructional changes in a timely fashion.

The first chapter of this book presents an overview of authentic assessment, where it came from and where it is going. The next four chapters focus on authentic assessments that can be used across the curriculum: portfolios, performance assessment, rubrics, and observation-based assessment. Then you will find a chapter that focuses on the inclusion of students and parents in the assessment process. The final four chapters identify authentic assessments that can be used specifically with each of the four content areas: language arts, math, science, and social studies. The book concludes with an extensive bibliography of authentic assessment resources and professional organizations. Enjoy!

Overview of Authentic Assessment

What is Authentic Assessment?

"Not everything that counts can be counted and not everything that can be counted counts." It has been alleged that this quote hung on the wall of Albert Einstein's office. It is important because it encapsulates the basic philosophy of authentic assessment. Authentic assessment is the process of gathering evidence and documenting a student's learning and growth in an authentic context. More and more teachers are adopting the philosophy that instruction and learning should be authentic. These teachers have embraced the whole language philosophy and use thematic units to teach grade level skills. As our instructional practices change to focus on authentic activities, our assessments must become more authentic as well. It would be completely inconsistent to adopt the whole language philosophy, and then use a basal reader multiple choice exam to test students' reading abilities. Standardized and multiple choice tests no longer fit the needs of progressive classrooms.

Authentic assessment, unlike traditional assessment, is used to evaluate the individual student. The student's work is compared to his or her previous work, rather than compared to the work of others, in

> **Authentic assessment is the process of gathering evidence and documenting a student's learning and growth in an authentic context.**

1

order to measure growth and progress. Student work is often collected in a portfolio, one of the most common methods of authentic assessment. The work in the portfolio is then reviewed periodically by teachers, students, and parents. A major goal of authentic assessment is to involve the students and parents in the assessment process. Although many teachers have been using the basic principles of authentic assessment for years, we have only recently acknowledged the importance and value of alternative forms of assessment and teachers' intuitive judgments about students.

Authentic assessment is based on what the child actually does, in a variety of contexts, at points throughout the school year. Authentic samples of student work are collected to serve as indicators of the child's growth and progress. These samples are authentic, meaning they represent the student's application, not mere acquisition, of knowledge and skills. For example, a multiple choice grammar test does not tell us much about a student writer. Having the student write an original story tells us much more about the student's competence as a writer. Yet, having only one story, while telling us more than a multiple choice test, still does not give us a complete picture of the child's ability as a writer. Several samples, in several genres, collected at several points of the year, are necessary for accurate assessment. The judgments we make based on the student samples are limited by the quality and quantity of the samples collected. No single test, single observation, or single piece of student work could possibly capture the continuous, multi-dimensional, interactive requirement of sound authentic assessment (Valencia, 1990b).

The judgments we make based on the student samples are limited by the quality and quantity of the samples collected.

Authentic assessment methods serve a dual purpose for teachers. Not only do these methods keep us well informed and provide concrete documentation about student's progress, they also help inform our curricular decisions. By making assessment an on-going, continuous process, we are in a better position to make decisions regarding lessons, skills, and curriculum goals. We, at any moment, can assess a student's progress by reviewing the portfolio contents and then determine if we need to review certain skills or repeat lessons based on student needs. The on-going process of authentic assessment means that we no longer have to wait until the end of an instructional unit before assessing a student's understanding of skills and concepts.

There are several methods of authentic assessment currently being used. Portfolios are probably the most popular method of authentic assessment. However, rubrics and performance assessment are quickly gaining ground. Observation-based assessment, including checklists and anecdotal records, is also being used by teachers as a means of documenting progress. The method you choose ultimately depends on the needs of your students. Remember, however, to start small. Choose one method for one curricular area. Then, as you become comfortable with the process, add other curriculum areas and other methods. Authentic assessment thus becomes beneficial for your students, without frustrating you in the process.

Standardized Tests

As early as 1845 Horace Mann suggested administering tests with large numbers of questions and the standardization of answers. Well over a century later, schools throughout the country administer anywhere from one, to upwards of three or four standardized tests each school year, taking away valuable instructional time. Standardized tests can be mandated at the school, district, and also state level. Standardized tests are used to determine how groups of students are performing in comparison with other groups (Seely, 1994). They serve a completely different purpose than authentic assessment. Authentic assessments tell us how well students can apply their knowledge; standardized tests are more efficient for determining how well students have acquired basic facts (Herman, Aschbacher, & Winters, 1992).

Authentic assessments tell us how well students can apply their knowledge; standardized tests are more efficient for determining how well students have acquired basic facts.

Why are standardized tests still used so frequently in schools? There are several reasons for this. First, they are extremely easy to administer. A standardized test can be administered to the entire class at one time. Also, because these tests are multiple choice with answers recorded on scantron forms, they are very easy to score. This method of scoring makes the tests relatively inexpensive because a machine, rather than a human, does all the scoring. Standardized tests also allow teachers, administrators, and parents to compare each student's score to those of other students at the same grade level.

Generally speaking, because standardized tests are objective the scores are considered very reliable. However, this is not necessarily the case. Let's say, for example, a fourth grade student receives a raw score of 53 on a standardized reading test. That raw score is then converted to a grade equivalent score of 4.7, meaning that the child's reading level is fourth grade, seventh month. However, every standardized test has a standard error of measurement. The standard error of measurement for this particular test is 2.7. That means the student's raw score could adjust either up or down as much as 2.7 points. This translates to a raw score that falls somewhere between 50.3 and 55.7. These scores convert to a grade equivalent in the range of 4.2 to 5.3. So, all we really know is that this student is reading somewhere between the fourth and fifth grade level. When the standard error of measurement is considered, the standardized test scores do not seem as accurate and reliable as they are sometimes portrayed. This inaccuracy can have serious ramifications for students.

The results of standardized tests are often critical to the student's instructional program. Students who have trouble mastering the basics tested may be placed in remedial groups or classes. How does this affect students of other cultures and languages? Difference in cultural knowledge and language can affect performance on standardized tests and therefore a disproportionate number of these students can end up in remedial classes when they need not be there at all.

> **Difference in cultural knowledge and language can affect performance on standardized tests and therefore a disproportionate number of these students can end up in remedial classes when they need not be there at all.**

In spite of their pitfalls, standardized tests probably will not be eliminated any time soon. Therefore, it is up to us to supplement these scores with concrete data that truly expresses the student's growth and progress throughout the school year by using authentic assessment.

Teacher Empowerment

Teachers often feel powerless in the face of standardized tests. These tests are developed by someone completely disconnected with the daily activities of the classroom, yet the results of the tests are used to make decisions that can dramatically affect the classroom. Instructional practices, student placement, and teacher accountability often rest upon the results of these standardized tests.

Authentic assessment methods provide a new role for teachers. We are now placed in the role of experts rather than technicians (Tierney, Carter, & Desai, 1991). As experts we must learn to trust our own judgments about students. We are, after all, in the best position to make such judgments. Unlike the invisible test writer, we are with our students everyday observing them as they use language, interact with other students, solve problems, and complete instructional tasks. We can see growth and progress over time because authentic assessment is an on-going process. As professionals we must trust our intuition about the students we know so well and the assessments we make of their achievements.

Taking on the role of expert brings a new responsibility to teachers. We must stay informed about curriculum and assessment. We must join professional organizations and read professional journals in order to stay current. The bibliography provides addresses for the following professional organizations: Association for Supervision and Curriculum Development, International Reading Association, National Council for the Social Studies, National Council for Teachers of Mathematics, and the National Science Teachers Association. If we want administrators and parents to trust our professional judgments, we must remain highly qualified and informed at all times.

Authentic Assessment Pilot Projects

Several states are currently piloting authentic assessment projects in their schools. The following is an overview of several states' efforts to implement authentic assessment. Vermont is often considered a leader in assessment because of their efforts to put in place a systematic assessment of student work through portfolios (Goldman, 1989). The Arizona Student Assessment Program requires that provisions be made for performance-based integrated assessments that measure broad outcomes and processes, as well as match the state's curriculum framework. The California State Department of Education has recently developed the *California Learning Record* (California State Department of Education, 1993). It is based on the *Primary Language Record* (Barrs, Ellis, Hester, & Thomas, 1991) developed at the Centre for Language in Primary Education in London, England. The purpose of the *Learning Record* is to assess students' abilities in reading, writing, listening, and speaking in authentic contexts. Last, but not least, New York, Florida, and New Hampshire are also in the process of implementing authentic assessment pilot projects in their schools.

Connecting Instruction and Assessment

Genuine evaluation is based on skills and knowledge developed throughout a course of study. Therefore, assessment tasks should look very similar to instructional tasks because assessment and instruction are inherently linked.

By connecting instruction and assessment, you eliminate those disengaging moments when the learning has to stop so the testing can begin (Perrone, 1991). Take, for example, science instruction that involves students actively in hands-on investigations. The passive quality of a multiple choice test disrupts the instructional flow because it is clearly seen as a separate activity (Perrone, 1991). Many teachers have become motivated about authentic assessment because they are tired of juggling instruction and assessment and trying to accommodate what are often competing goals (Valencia, 1990a).

5

Assessment and instructional practices should be seen as influencing and driving each other (Seely, 1994). Unfortunately, too often assessment is treated as completely separate from instruction. Students are tested following the completion of a unit of study, and often times they have no idea what they will be tested on. With this method, students don't know how well they are doing until the instructional unit is complete. By that time it is too late to seek clarification of concepts not well understood. Furthermore, because the unit of study is complete, students are less likely to review material in order to reach a level of understanding necessary for mastery. When assessment is on-going, as is the case with authentic assessment, teachers and students are in a position to evaluate the learning process throughout the course of the study. If there is confusion about something, a lesson can be created to clarify the misunderstanding or misconception before it is too late to make a difference. Now assessment serves a dual purpose; to provide teachers with information about students' achievements and also to provide knowledge for curricular decision making.

When assessment is on-going, as is the case with authentic assessment, teachers and students are in a position to evaluate the learning process throughout the course of the study.

Sound authentic assessment forces you to clearly define your instructional goals because assessment criteria must be explicit. In the process of selecting and defining your assessment criteria, you are also selecting and defining your instructional goals. Because instruction and assessment are so closely linked, our assessment methods must closely target our instructional aims in order for students to showcase their achievements. If, for example, our instructional goal is to have students apply the scientific method by completing an experiment, we must teach them this process. The assessment, then, must require students to perform an experiment using the process. A multiple choice exam about an experiment would be completely inappropriate. The assessment task must match the instructional objective it is designed to measure (Herman, Aschbacher, & Winters, 1992). Authentic assessment also encourages higher standards for instruction because the high standards for learning contained in the assessment become those for instruction as well (Parker, 1991).

Concluding Remarks

As our classroom activities become more authentic, so must our assessment practices. If we want to teach our students to write, then we must allow them to write. If we want to assess their writing skills, we should review their writing samples collected, perhaps, in a portfolio. Authentic assessment allows us the opportunity to evaluate each child's ability individually based on evidence of their growth and progress over a period of time.

Portfolio Assessment

Background Information

Portfolios are collections of student work reviewed against criteria in order to assess students' progress over time. The "assessment" in portfolio assessment only exists when the assessment purpose is defined and the criteria for what to put in the portfolio and how it will be evaluated are identified and explicit (Herman, Aschbacher, & Winters, 1992). Portfolios were the first type of authentic assessment to gain ground. Portfolios represent a philosophy that demands we view assessment as an integral part of our instruction, providing a vehicle for teachers and students to use as a guide for learning. This is an expanded view of assessment in which a variety of indicators of learning are gathered across many situations before, during, and after instruction. It is a philosophy that honors both the process and the products of learning, as well as the active participation of the teacher and the students in their own evaluation and growth (Valencia, 1990b).

Portfolios represent a philosophy that demands we view assessment as an integral part of our instruction, providing a vehicle for teachers and students to use as a guide for learning.

In the Beginning

Artists, models, and photographers rely on portfolios to demonstrate their skills and achievements. Within the portfolio they include samples of their work that exemplify the depth and breadth of their expertise (Valencia, 1990b). Not all work in the portfolio has reached completion, and there may be works at several stages of the process. The portfolio may contain several types of works using several types of medium collected over an artist's career. The contents of the portfolio changes as the artist changes and grows. The key point is that the portfolio is not a static entity, rather it is an ever-growing, ever-changing reflection of ability and achievement.

Portfolios Today

Portfolios have gained popularity in the wake of the concept that assessment should be authentic, on-going, and collaborative. It should be authentic, meaning that assessment should accurately and realistically paint a picture of how the child is progressing, using examples of activities that the child is working on in his or her daily classroom experiences. Children, like adults, are constantly changing and growing. This is precisely the reason assessment needs to be on-going. The active process by the teacher and student in choosing, adding, and deleting contents of the portfolio is an integral part of the portfolio concept because it reflects the belief that learning is on-going and therefore, never complete (Goodman, Bird, & Goodman, 1992). With both the teacher and the student participating in the selection of the contents of the portfolio, assessment becomes a collaborative process.

> **With both the teacher and student participating in the selection of the contents of the portfolio, assessment becomes a collaborative process.**

Where Do I Start?

Beginning a portfolio system in your class can seem like an insurmountable task. However, if you begin with just one area of the curriculum you will see that it's not only easy to use portfolios, but fun as well. Once you have become comfortable with using portfolios in that one curricular area, you can begin to add others. Language arts is an easy place to begin because writing lends itself so well to portfolio assessment. Yet, if you feel more comfortable with math, science, or social studies, those areas will work just as well. The important thing to remember is to have confidence in yourself and your ability to choose what is appropriate for the needs of your students.

After you have selected the area of the curriculum for which you will use portfolios, you can begin making other important decisions. First, you should define your purpose for using portfolios. Based on your purpose you can determine the type of portfolio your students will use; a collection portfolio, a showcase portfolio, or a teacher assessment portfolio. Once you know the type of portfolio you will use you can take the most important step, setting criteria.

Remember, a folder with a collection of work is a portfolio, but portfolio assessment only exists when the criteria for evaluation has been clearly defined. After the criteria is set you can collect student samples. There is a wide range of items that can be included in the portfolio. You will find some suggestions later in this chapter. Finally, you will evaluate the portfolio using your predetermined criteria, and then report the results to the student and parent. All four of these steps, defining your purpose, setting criteria, collecting samples, and evaluation and reporting, are discussed in greater detail below.

Defining the Purpose

The first step in using portfolios in your classroom is to define their purpose. The purpose will depend on the assessment needs of your class. Defining your purpose early will help you to make decisions regarding what area of the curriculum to begin with, what type of portfolio to use, how many samples to save, and how to organize the portfolio. Use the following questions to help you establish the purpose for portfolios in your classroom. Will the portfolio be a collection of work or a sample of the student's best work? Will the portfolio house finished products only? Will the portfolio be passed on to the next teacher? Who will select what to include in the portfolio? Who will have access to the portfolio? How will students be involved with the portfolio?

After you have answered those basic questions, you can begin to think about some deeper issues regarding portfolio assessment such as what aspects of student performance you need to know about and how you plan to use the results. (Herman, Aschbacher, & Winters, 1992). If your interest is in the acquisition and application of knowledge and skills, you will want to look at the products of student learning. If your interest is in diagnosis and improvement of student strengths and needs, you will want to look at the process of student learning. Once you have analyzed these aspects of student performance, you can use the results to guide instruction, document progress over time, or to supplement standardized test scores.

Types of Portfolios

There are many kinds of portfolios. The type of portfolio you ultimately decide to use in your classroom depends on your particular assessment needs. It is important to remember that decisions regarding the type of portfolio to use in your classroom are not etched in stone. Many teachers try several different types of portfolios before settling on the one that works best for them and their students.

Many teachers try several different types of portfolios before settling on the one that works best for them and their students.

Although there are many types of portfolios, the most common fall into one of four categories: the collection portfolio, the showcase or display portfolio, the assessment portfolio, and the teacher professional portfolio (Jasmine, 1993). The collection portfolio is a folder that holds an accumulation of a student's work. The showcase or display portfolio is a selection of work that represents a student's progress and achievements. This portfolio is commonly shown at report card time or at Open House. The assessment portfolio is a collection of documentation used to support or supplement the student's report card grade. The teacher professional portfolio is a record of your own growth, learning, and professional progress as a teacher during the school year. In some schools principals are requiring teachers to keep their own portfolios to share at the yearly performance review. However, even when not required to do so, many teachers are beginning to keep their own portfolios alongside those of their students (Hill & Ruptic, 1994). Suggestions for what to include in each of the portfolios described are highlighted below.

In some schools principals are requiring teachers to keep their own portfolios to share at the yearly performance review.

Collection Portfolio:

  writing samples at all stages of the writing process
  reading inventories and checklists
  tapes of oral reading
  math problem-solving samples

Showcase or Display Portfolio:

  items from the collection portfolio
  student self-reflections
  personal items such as photos, awards, and other memorabilia

Assessment Portfolio:

  samples of work
  anecdotal records
  student-teacher conference reports

Teacher Professional Portfolio:

  samples of student work
  samples of units you created
  articles from professional journals
  notes or certificates from in-services, workshops, or conferences

Setting Criteria

The need for standards is another consideration when adopting the use of portfolios. We must have criteria against which to judge the quality of the work in the portfolio. Having established criteria will greatly help you when report card time rolls around. You can use the criteria to review the contents of the portfolio and determine a formal grade, if your school requires that you give grades. Some schools are moving toward a narrative-type report card in which single grades give way to brief essays regarding students' progress. With this type of grading system, portfolios become an invaluable part of student assessment.

In the past, assessment was done "by" the teacher "to" the student. The results of this assessment were reported to students and parents by means of a single grade on a quarterly report card. Yet, how many times has a student asked you why he received a certain grade? Or, has a parent ever expressed concern to you because he felt his daughter was doing well, yet her grade did not reflect such progress? These situations occur because grading criteria are often a mystery to both students and parents. Portfolio assessment attempts to demystify the grading process by making public the assessment criteria. Students are aware of the expectations required of them because they know the assessment criteria from the start.

Portfolio assessment attempts to demystify the grading process by making public the assessment criteria.

The best way to establish the criteria for evaluating portfolios is for you to determine if you want to do a quantitative or qualitative assessment. A quantitative assessment merely evaluates the quantity of items included in the portfolio. This may be a good starting point for teachers and students because it is very easy to do. The teacher, with input from the students, creates a list if items required to be in the portfolio. From this list a checklist is generated that students can put inside their portfolios to assist with record keeping. A sample portfolio checklist can be found on page 13. As they place items in their portfolio, they can check it off on the list. This allows both you and the student to see at an instant what is left to be included in order to meet the quantitative requirements. Another reason that starting with a quantitative assessment is beneficial is because it helps get students in the habit of putting things in their portfolio, something we need to train them to do. It would be very frustrating for you to begin a portfolio evaluation and then find that the items you specified to be included are not there.

To do a quantitative evaluation of the portfolio you simply check to see that all items specified for inclusion are there. You are not judging the quality of the items included, only their presence. Once you and the students are comfortable with the quantitative evaluation process, you can either add a qualitative analysis, or use the qualitative evaluation in place of the quantitative.

The portfolio qualitative evaluation is accomplished by means of a grading criteria sheet, or rubric. The rubric defines scoring criteria explicitly for you and the students. You may develop the rubric yourself, or you can allow students to give their input. A sample rubric for a writing portfolio can be found on page 14. Rubrics can be of great assistance to you in maintaining consistency of grading. Evaluating portfolios is obviously subjective. However, when criteria are explicit you can be confident that there will be a high level of consistency in grading. For more detailed information on rubrics, see chapter four.

Grading criteria may change as expectations for students change.

Grading criteria may change as expectations for students change. Consequently, you and your students may have to develop new rubrics periodically throughout the school year. Remember that determining the criteria should be a joint effort between you and your students whenever possible. The more involved and aware students are regarding grading criteria, the better prepared they are to meet your expectations and standards.

Collection Portfolio Contents Checklist

This collection portfolio is the property of

_____

It contains samples of my work in these subject areas:

❑ Writing _____

_____

_____

❑ Math _____

_____

_____

❑ Social Studies _____

_____

_____

❑ Science _____

_____

_____

❑ Art/Music _____

_____

_____

Reprinted from TCM506 Middle School Assessment, *Teacher Created Materials, 1994*

RUBRIC FOR
WRITING PORTFOLIOS

Score 3:

Writing samples demonstrate mature and original use of language.

Writing samples demonstrate developed ideas.

Writing samples demonstrate skills in organization and mechanics.

Score 2:

Writing samples demonstrate competent use of language.

Writing samples show fairly well-developed ideas.

Writing samples demonstrate some skill in organization and mechanics.

Score 1:

Writing samples partially suggests competent use of language.

Writing samples show little or no sign of original ideas.

Writing samples contain major weaknesses in organization and mechanics.

Portfolio Houses

Once you have set your criteria students can begin collecting samples. You can use basic manila folders housed in hanging files, or you can create personalized portfolios for each student. Below are some portfolio ideas, along with explanations and illustrations. Choose what you think will work best for your students based on the types of items you want included in the portfolio.

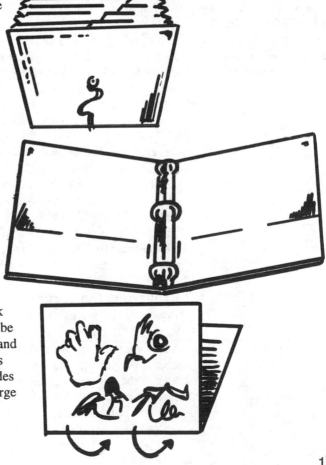

Students can color their own manila folder. These folders can be stored in hanging files.

Students can be given their own expandable files. Sections can be labeled for each subject area as well as for reflections, work in progress, and thematic projects.

Small expandable files can be placed inside a large binder. Students can personalize the files, but the binder is numbered and can therefore be used from year to year.

Posterboard can be folded to look like a folder. Then the front can be decorated with a student picture and hand prints. This portfolio works particularly well for primary grades because students often include large objects and pictures.

Some less expensive options may be to use large envelopes, perhaps even X-ray envelopes if they are available to you from a local hospital. For odd shaped objects such as audiotapes and videotapes, a pizza box can serve as the portfolio. They are inexpensive (often free) and easy to store because they are stackable. Use any of these portfolio ideas or a combination of ideas to house student samples.

Collecting Samples

It is necessary to choose a basic list of requirements you will want to collect for each student's portfolio. You may choose to base this list on your district standards, school goals, grade level curriculum, or the specific needs of your own classroom as determined by you and your students.

> **There are certainly many possibilities to consider when deciding what to include in the portfolio; and this is precisely what makes portfolios so versatile.**

There are certainly many possibilities to consider when deciding what to include in the portfolio; and this is precisely what makes portfolios so versatile. The flexibility of the portfolio allows you and your students to set the limits according to your needs. The student should not only be allowed, but also encouraged to assist in this decision making process. You may, however, find it helpful at evaluation time if you have required students to include some process, as well as product samples. This will allow you, the student, and the parent, to discuss progress based not only on the final product, but also on the student's process for getting there.

The challenge in determining what to include in the portfolio is making sure you have enough data, but not so much that it is overwhelming to evaluate. The key is to have a variety of assignments, collected at different times during the semester or quarter, showing both process and product. Remember, any single item is only a minuscule sample of a student's accomplishments. The more information included, the more complete the picture of the student's progress (Anthony, Johnson, Mickelson, & Preece, 1991).

Evaluating the Portfolio

Take time to review the portfolio before doing your analysis. Perhaps even note some brief comments about strengths and needs. Allow yourself time with the portfolio so a complete picture of the student can emerge. Review portfolio selections using your knowledge of the subject area, class expectations, and your understanding of the strengths and needs of the particular student (Tierney, Carter, & Desai, 1991). Certainly this process will be time consuming. For this reason, you may want to limit the number of items to include in the portfolio, at least at first.

For the quantitative evaluation, determine whether or not students have met your requirements for what to include in the portfolio. In other words, did the student have the two writing assignments, conference report, and research project you required? The student's record keeping checklist will be of great assistance to you for the quantitative analysis. The student's score or grade is simply based on the number of required items they collected in their portfolio.

For the qualitative evaluation you will use the grading criteria rubric to determine the grade. An accompanying narrative report is appropriate for commenting on student performance and progress. In the narrative report, you analyze to what extent the student met the established grading criteria as defined in the rubric. Be prepared to give specific comments to students regarding their strengths and areas that need improvement. On page 18 you can find a narrative form to use for qualitative analysis of a social studies portfolio.

In the process of reviewing portfolios and diagnosing individual needs and strengths, you may find that some students are having difficulty with a specific skill.

In the process of reviewing portfolios and diagnosing individual needs and strengths, you may find that some students are having difficulty with a specific skill. You can then use this information when planning your curriculum. In this way your assessment procedures are guiding your instruction. After designing lessons to assist students in the acquisition of the specific skill, you can collect a new sample from students. Now you can compare the two samples and review student progress over time. You can also use the samples in the portfolio to supplement standardized test scores. For example, standardized tests provide information on writing mechanics, yet do not require students to create original discourse. The writing samples collected in the portfolio can supplement the mechanics scores with information about the content and structure of student writing. Now the teacher, student, and parent have a more complete picture of that child as a writer.

The results of the portfolio evaluation should be discussed with both students and parents during the assessment conference. At this time you can discuss student achievement in relation to the established scoring criteria. This procedure gives students and parents far more information than they receive from report card grades. For more information on conferencing, see chapter six "Involving Students and Parents in Assessment."

Portfolio Content Analysis

Student's Name _____ Date_____

Classroom Work

Research Projects

Cooperative Investigations

Written Products

Self-Evaluations

Reprinted from TCM780 Social Studies Assessment, *Teacher Created Materials, 1994*

Students and the Portfolio

With portfolio assessment the teacher and student are no longer enemies in the grading process. Instead, they are partners in the learning and evaluation process. The student should take a very active role in defining criteria, selecting samples, and even evaluating the portfolio. Brainstorming portfolio criteria makes students feel as though they have some power in the assessment process. They will also better understand criteria they have participated in selecting and defining. Students should also participate in the selection of pieces to include in the portfolio. Encourage the student to include those pieces of work that he/she feels are the best reflection of his/her progress throughout the grading period. In making decisions for what to include in the portfolio, students must become thoughtful judges of their own work and reflect on their own progress. The recognition of the student's ownership of the papers, evaluation, and the learning process is crucial to the success of the portfolio approach.

After the student selects several samples for the portfolio, he/she should reflect on those pieces.

Student self-evaluation, as well as teacher evaluation of portfolio selections, is a crucial part of the portfolio "partnership." After the student selects several samples for the portfolio, he/she should reflect on those pieces. The student could respond to questions such as: Why did you choose this sample for the portfolio? How does this piece reflect your progress and growth? What do you like best about this piece? Older students can respond to these questions on their own in writing. Younger students can conference with you or a parent volunteer. You can record their answers to the prompts by transcribing exactly what the student says. You should attach these written reflections to the appropriate sample and include them in the portfolio. A sample student reflection form can be found on page 45.

Parents and the Portfolio

Portfolios, unlike the quarterly report card, inform parents of their child's on-going growth throughout the school year. The type of concrete, empirical data contained in the portfolio will give parents evidence of their child's progress. This concrete date can be used to supplement the report card grade, or standardized test scores which are often reported to parents during conferences. Also, because the portfolio is cumulative, it is easy to refer to earlier samples of student work when discussing the progress made. If parents are provided with this evolving description of their child's development over time, they will be less likely to put undue value on report card grades and standardized test scores (Harp, 1993).

It is not necessary to wait until report card time to inform parents of their child's progress. You may want to establish a regular schedule for sending home student portfolios for parents to review. You can invite them to respond to the portfolio in writing or create a form that addresses specific information you would like the parent to provide. The key is to keep the parent as informed as possible regarding their child's growth and progress.

Concluding Remarks

Portfolios are no longer only for artists and craftsmen. Students and teachers are keeping their own portfolios to display their growth and progress. The first step to portfolio assessment implementation is to define the purpose for the use of portfolios. Once this decision has been made you can decide on the appropriate type of portfolios to use: the collection portfolio, the showcase portfolio, or the assessment portfolio. Teachers can even keep their own professional portfolios. The second step is to set criteria, either qualitative or quantitative. The third step is to collect students samples. The final step is to evaluate the portfolio based on your established criteria.

Involving students and parents in the portfolio process is an important step. If you want students to take ownership of the portfolio, then they must be allowed to participate in some of the decision making in regards to the portfolio. Parents can be invited to view the portfolio throughout the year, not just at report card time. Involving students and parents completes the assessment cycle because all three participants: the teacher, the parent, and the student are directly involved.

Performance Assessment

Background Information

Performance assessment requires students to actively accomplish complex and significant tasks, while bringing to bear prior knowledge, recent learning, and relevant skills to solve realistic problems (Herman, Aschbacher, & Winters, 1992). For example, if you design a writing assignment in which you ask your students to write letters to the editor of a local newspaper that has published an article criticizing your school, you have created a tool for performance assessment. This type of assessment allows students to demonstrate their understanding of concepts and to apply knowledge and skills they have acquired. Performance assessment tasks are carefully constructed in order to assess specific knowledge along with critical thinking skills. They can be used in all areas of the curriculum.

In constructing tasks to assess specific knowledge of a topic you should make an effort to incorporate critical thinking skills. In order to focus on higher order thinking, ask students to compare, classify, and analyze data rather than just regurgitate information. The performance tasks are the scored based on grading rubrics that are, in many cases, established by the teacher prior to the task. However,

> **Performance assessment tasks are carefully constructed in order to assess specific declarative and procedural knowledge along with critical thinking skills.**

21

when appropriate, students should be encouraged to participate in establishing the rubric. This allows them some ownership of the assessment process. The most important principle to remember is that the task and the rubric should be established and discussed clearly with students prior to engagement in the activity.

Performance Task Types

There are twelve basic types of performance tasks that you can use to assess knowledge, as well as critical thinking skills. A **comparison task** requires students to compare two or more people, places, or things. For example, students can compare the protagonists from two separate stories they have read in class. A **classification task** asks students to classify, or put into categories, certain people, places, or things. For example, in science you may ask students to classify animals according to their habitats. A **position support task** asks the student to take a position on a subject or issue and defend that position. As part of a unit on the Constitution, students could consider the issue of gun control and the second amendment, and then write a statement of their position on the issue. An **application task** asks students to apply knowledge in a new situation. This task lends itself well to writing. Students can read a number of fairy tales and identify the common elements of this type of story. Then, using this knowledge they write a fairy tale of their own. In an **analyzing perspective task** students analyze two to three different perspectives, and then choose a perspective to support. As a social studies task, students can analyze the perspectives of the environmentalists and the Brazilians regarding rain forest destruction. A sample of this task is located on page 25. In a **decision making task** students must identify the factors that caused a certain decision to be made. This task works well in reader's response. Students can identify the factors that caused a character to make a certain decision. The **historical perspective task** asks students to consider differing theories to answer basic historical questions. For example, students might consider the theories for why and how dinosaurs became extinct. A **predictive task** requires students to make predictions about what could have happened or will happen in the future. A mathematics predictive task may ask students to predict if a coin tossed ten times will land most often as heads or tails. With the **problem solving task** students must create a solution to a specific problem. An example of a mathematics problem solving task would ask students to select the fewest number of coins to equal 56 cents. An **experimental task** requires students to set up an experiment to test a hypothesis. Students in a science class may set up an experiment to see if a certain plant will grow better with sunlight or in the dark. The **invention task** asks students to create something new and

> **There are twelve basic types of performance tasks that you can use to assess declarative and procedural knowledge, as well as critical thinking skills.**

unique. As part of a unit on holidays, students can invent a special symbol for any national holiday of their choice. Lastly, the **error identification task** asks students to identify specific errors or misrepresentations. A task example could be to have a community policeman come to the class and discuss his/her job. Then, students can watch a television show about police and identify things the policemen did on the television show that they did not believe accurately portrayed what a real policeman would do.

Writing the Task

The first step in creating a performance task is to determine what content knowledge you wish to assess. A basic premise underlying the construction of performance tasks is that they require an application of content knowledge.

Next, you must determine the type of performance task you will use to assess the content knowledge. Twelve types of performance tasks are described along with examples under the heading "Performance Task Types." Choose the task that most strongly emphasizes the content knowledge you wish to assess.

Once you have made all the decisions described above you can begin writing the performance task. The construction of a performance task can be a time consuming process. However, with practice the tasks become easier to write. An added benefit is that you can use the tasks from one year to the next so you will not have to create a whole new set of tasks each school year. Also, you need not take the entire responsibility of writing the performance tasks on your own. Other grade level teachers can be solicited to assist in this process. In doing so, you establish consistency of expectations for your entire grade level. The actual writing of the task is similar to writing a well-crafted composition (Marzano, Pickering, & McTighe, 1993). Consequently, it may take several drafts before you reach a level of satisfaction.

When writing the task, you should include some basic background information for students along with any other pertinent information you feel they may need. You may also wish to include an activity sheet that students can use to help them organize their thoughts, ideas, and research. The task should also include a detailed description of the way in which the students will present their findings or answers. Some presentation ideas may include a written report, a letter to an official, a dramatization, or an oral report, to name just a few. The performance task should always be discussed clearly with students prior to the activity. Student responses to the task are

> **The construction of a performance task can be a time consuming process. However, with practice the tasks become easier to write.**

scored according to a rubric, also explicitly defined and discussed prior to the activity. Detailed information on rubrics is described in the next chapter.

Responses to performance tasks can be included in the student's portfolio. Be sure to have the established rubrics handy when sharing performance task responses with parents. The rubric will clearly show how you arrived at the student's score for the task. It will also show your expectations for the task. If you feel you need to more explicitly illustrate expectations for parents, you can use anchor papers. Anchor papers are those selected that represent each score on the rubric. So, you would have an anchor paper example to illustrate a score 3, score 2, and score 1. To protect the confidentiality of your students, use papers from students in another class, and be sure to remove the student's name from the anchor paper. The anchor papers can also be made available to students to serve as examples of your expectations for the task.

If you feel you need to more explicitly illustrate expectations for parents, you can use anchor papers. Anchor papers are those selected that represent each score on the rubric.

On the pages that follow you will find an example of an analyzing perspective task and a visual representation sheet to assist students in organizing their thoughts for this specific task. A rubric for this task can be found on page 30 in the chapter on rubrics. This analyzing perspectives task is appropriate for students at the fifth, sixth, or seventh grade level.

Concluding Remarks

There are a variety of performance tasks available to use with your students. Consequently, performance tasks can be used with every area of the curriculum. The tasks are scored using rubrics, or scoring guides, established prior to students' engagement in the activity. The rubric makes your expectations and standards for the performance task explicit.

Writing performance tasks can take some time. However, after writing several tasks, this process becomes much easier. Keep in mind, once you have written the task it can be used with students for years to come.

Analyzing Perspectives Task

Background Information:

Rain forest destruction has become big news in recent years. Many people worry about the future of the Amazon rain forest in Brazil if deforestation is allowed to continue there. Brazilians living in this rapidly diminishing country are concerned with their country's economic well-being.

Differing Perspectives:

The United States has many powerful environmental activist groups that are sincerely concerned about rain forest destruction. According to some estimates, every second of every day we are losing a tropical rain forest the size of a football field. Activists contend that when forests go, so do animals, plants, insects, and birds.

Brazilians have a different perspective on the same issue. Brazil has a large and rapidly growing population. Providing jobs for this large population is paramount to the country's economic well being. Brazil's exports include cattle and lumber. Forests are cleared so that cattle can graze and to provide lumber to export. The use of the rain forest is necessary to raise the standard of living of Brazilians.

Your Task:

You have been provided with two different perspectives regarding the Amazon rain forest in Brazil. Consider the motivations behind each of the two perspectives such as economic motivation, emotional motivation, and cultural motivation. Use the visual representation sheet to help you organize this information. After you have analyzed the perspectives determine your own position on this issue. Write a position statement presenting your opinion, what information you have based that opinion on, and what specifically made you choose that opinion.

Reprinted from TCM780 Social Studies Assessment, *Teacher Created Materials, 1994*

Visual Representation

Name _____

Date _____

	Environmental Activist	Brazilian
Position on rain forest issue		
Motivation for position on rain forest		

Your opinion:

_____

_____

_____

_____

_____

_____

_____

Reprinted from TCM780 Social Studies Assessment, *Teacher Created Materials, 1994*

Rubrics

What is a Rubric?

A rubric is a set of criteria students see prior to engaging in a task. The rubric can be established for a single task, such as a performance task or a writing assignment, or for several tasks that may be collected in the portfolio. A writing portfolio rubric example can be found on page 14. The rubric identifies the qualities the teacher expects to see in responses at several points along a scale (Valencia, Hiebert, & Afflerbach, 1994). Each score on the rubric is matched to an example of a response. By viewing established criteria prior to the activity, students clearly know what is expected in order to receive a specific score.

> By viewing established criteria prior to the activity, students clearly know what is expected in order to receive a specific score.

There are two types of rubrics: analytic and holistic. A holistic rubric is used to measure the overall quality of a student response. In writing, a holistic rubric is used to judge the overall organization, creativity, and expression of ideas. An analytic rubric is used to measure specific aspects of the work. In writing, an analytic rubric may be used to assess sentence structure, capitalization, and punctuation. Students receive two separate scores based on the holistic and analytic rubric. You can use these rubrics together because they

27

measure different things. For example, you might score an essay holistically for all your students and analytically only for those who did not meet your expectations related to basic mechanics skills.

Writing a Rubric

The rubric is established prior to students engaging in the task or collecting samples for a portfolio. Your rubric may have between three and six categories of responses, the decision in many cases based on the grade level you teach. A three point rubric is the most common for two reasons. First of all, a three point rubric is fairly easy to write because you are identifying descriptors for an average response, above average response, and below average response. Also, it is easy to score student papers using a three point rubric because the distinctions between the three scores are very clear. When using a five or six point rubric, the gradations between scores are so slight that it makes difficult to determine the student's score. You may have a situation where you have difficulty determining if a paper is a four or five because the difference between the two is so slight. Some teachers find it easiest to use a four point rubric, particularly if they ultimately have to translate rubric scores into report card grades. Each point on the four point rubric can represent a grade of either A, B, C, or D. You choose the number of points on the rubric based on the needs of your particular class. However, if you ultimately decide to use a five or six point rubric, you should still introduce rubrics using a three point scale. After you and your students are comfortable with the three point scale, then you can advance to a more detailed rubric scale. Keep in mind when establishing rubrics that the burden for establishing criteria does not always have to rest upon the teacher alone. After students have had some experience with rubrics, their opinions can, and should be solicited prior to establishing the rubric. By helping to create a rubric, students become more aware of task expectations and may therefore perform better.

Prior to creating the rubric, you may find it helpful to collect student samples demonstrating a range of performance for the task or assignment. When reviewing these papers, consider the characteristics that distinguish a highly effective response from an effective response, and an effective response from an ineffective response. These characteristics become the descriptors for the rubric at each level. When using a three point rubric, the top score, or score three is for a student who demonstrates a thorough understanding. Score two is for students who show a complete and accurate understanding. The lowest score, or score one, is for students who demonstrate an incomplete understanding, or severe misconceptions.

> Keep in mind when establishing rubrics that the burden for establishing criteria does not always have to rest upon the teacher alone.

Similar to writing a performance task, a rubric may go through many drafts. After you write the rubric, test it with a particular assignment. Based on this trial test, you can adjust the criteria as necessary. Then, try it again to be sure that you feel comfortable with it as an accurate assessment tool.

Although it takes time to write rubrics, it is worth it because they serve a dual purpose. Along with serving as an assessment tool, a rubric can be a teaching tool as well. When a rubric is used as an assessment tool, it serves as a standard against which student work is judged. A rubric as a teaching tool provides a target for students. Anchor papers, or projects scored at each level of the rubric can be made available to students, thereby giving them access to the standards by which they are judged (Jasmine, 1994). These sample papers can be collected in a three ring binder and categorized according to each of the content areas. Not only will the students benefit from having access to these papers, but parents may want to see them as well if they have questions regarding your expectations and their child's ability to meet those expectations. On the following page you will find a sample rubric for the performance task described on page 25. An additional rubric example can be found on page 31. It is a six point rubric for mathematics.

Analyzing Perspectives Task Rubric

Score 3:

- The student clearly identifies the two positions on rain forests.
- The student clearly understands the motivations behind the two positions both explicit and implicit.
- The student clearly articulates his/her view on the rain forest issue with a strong line of reasoning to support it.

Score 2:

- The student has a basic understanding of the two rain forest perspectives.
- The student has a basic understanding of the motivations behind the two perspectives.
- The student articulates his/her view on the rain forest, but with little support.

Score 1:

- The student did not have a basic understanding of the two perspectives or their motivations.
- The student did not clearly articulate his/her opinion of the rain forest issue.

Score 0:

- The student did not respond to the task.

Reprinted from TCM780 Social Studies Assessment, *Teacher Created Materials, 1994*

Generalized Task Rubric

6 Exemplary Achievement

- Demonstrates deep understanding of major concepts
  - uses language to describe process or strategy
  - reflects and generalizes about process and purpose

5 Commendable Achievement

- Demonstrates detailed understanding of major concepts
  - uses language, to a point, to describe process or strategy
  - reflects and generalizes about process and purpose

4 Adequate Achievement

- Demonstrates a fundamental level of understanding of major concepts
  - uses language at the literal level
  - reflects about process and purpose

3 Some Evidence of Achievement

- Demonstrates partial understanding of the major concepts
  - is stronger at "doing" than at describing with language
  - solves basic problems at the concrete level only

2 Limited Evidence of Achievement

- Demonstrates a lack of required skills to complete task
  - attempts task but does not recognize "incorrect" solutions
  - hesitates to discuss any aspects of situation

1 Minimal Evidence of Achievement

- Demonstrates a lack of understanding of task
  - combines objects to create a set, but makes no connections to symbols or generalized process

0 No Participation or Response

Reprinted from TCM778 Math Assessment, *Teacher Created Materials, 1994*

Achieving Consistency with Rubrics

Scoring with rubrics, like other forms of authentic assessment, is very subjective. However, having well-defined, explicit criteria goes a long way toward achieving consistency in scoring with a rubric, in spite of its subjective nature.

One way to test the consistency of your rubric is by soliciting the assistance of fellow teachers. Given the rubric you created, along with several copies of students' papers representing each point on the scale, see if your colleagues score the papers the same way you did. If the score is the same, you can feel assured that your rubric will promote consistency in grading. If you find great variability among scores, consider making adjustments to your rubric. You may then choose to check this rubric once more prior to using it formally with students.

Once you become confident about the consistency of a particular rubric, save scored student samples to use in the future as anchor papers. Students can use anchor papers as examples of your expectations. Your colleagues may also want to use your anchor papers to assist them in establishing their own rubrics.

Concluding Remarks

Authentic assessment is often criticized because it is considered subjective. However, if rubrics are used consistent scoring can be achieved. The rubric clearly identifies the teacher's standards and expectations thereby making the grading criteria public. Students clearly know what is expected of them in order to receive a specific score. Rubrics can be used in any area of the curriculum. They can also be used to score a student's portfolio.

The rubric is always discussed with students in detail prior to engagement in the activity or task. Any questions students may have can be addressed at this time. You may also wish to share samples of other students' work representing each score on the rubric thereby making your criteria even more explicit for your students.

Observation-Based Assessment

Background Information

Observation-based assessment is a new name for something teachers have been doing for years. We have always observed our students, making mental and written notes about their progress. In the past, however, we kept these notes private and did not really consider them "assessment" per se. Recently, this has changed. Teachers are now trusting their judgments more than ever. Observation-based assessment brings with it recognition for and appreciation of the expertise of the classroom teacher (Jasmine, 1994).

There are two types of observations teachers can make: objective and interpretive. When using the objective style, you record what you are seeing as if you are a camera. Checklists are an objective form of observation because they require you to check off the skills or behaviors you observe. Anecdotal records, on the other hand, can be either objective or interpretive. The interpretive style goes beyond recording. With it you evaluate and comment on the notes you have taken. This may assist you in recognizing the implications of what you have observed.

There are two types of observations teachers can make: objective and interpretive.

Focused Observations

Naturally, we are observing students throughout the day as they participate in the learning process. This type of observation is considered unfocused. In other words, we are not observing any particular child for any particular reason.

Focused observations should be planned and key on a particular area of learning, or a particular student. As much as possible you should make note of precisely what the student is doing or saying, being as specific as you can. You may consider making note of the context in which the observation took place. It is also crucial to record the date along with the observation. Keep in mind when you are doing focused observations that your goal is to be a camera recording exactly what is happening. Leave the interpretation of your observation notes for another time. Also, refrain from offering any assistance to the child while making your observation.

When to Make Observations

Every day provides many opportunities to observe students. Recording your observations should not be disruptive to the normal flow of the classroom. Take advantage of "down time" to jot down notes or record marks on a checklist. Or, use the time when students are working independently to make and record your observations. Depending on the structure of your classroom activities, you may need to build observational time into your weekly schedule in order to assure that you will have the time to do it. Use classroom aides and parents to assist you so you can be sure this very important observational time is not shortchanged.

Your observations of students should take place in authentic situations with students doing authentic activities. The most powerful aspect of using observation as the basis of evaluation is that it can reflect the "real world" (Harp, 1993). Students should be observed in a variety of contexts doing a variety of activities. Observe them during instructional time, play time, reading with partners, and writing stories. If your intention is to base your evaluation on these observations, it is imperative that you have observed students in as many different contexts, as many different times as possible. Too few observations can be like evaluating a child based on a single test (Harp, 1993). As you observe students, make marks on a checklist or brief anecdotal records to indicate what you saw at that particular time.

Students should be observed in a variety of contexts doing a variety of activities.

Anecdotal Records

Anecdotal records are carefully documented notes of certain events, behaviors, and skills. They provide a record that you can review independently or share with parents during conference time. When your anecdotal notes are put together they tell an on-going story about students' growth and progress.

At the beginning of the year, it may be necessary to make more general entries as you start the process of becoming familiar with your students. You may also make notes about certain actions or behaviors to watch for in the future. As you get to know your students, your entries may become more specific or the types of entries may change.

When first beginning to use anecdotal records, you may find it easier to focus on only one curricular area. Or, perhaps you will focus on only one or two students for your observations. If you start out small and manageable, you are less likely to become frustrated with the process.

Managing Your Anecdotal Notes

There are several ways you can manage the anecdotal notes you take. Choose the method you think will work best for you. Yet, do not feel locked to this method if it does not work well. You may need to try several methods before settling on what makes you most comfortable and most productive.

A simple way to record your anecdotal records involves several copies of a recording form and a notebook. You may choose to have a form for each individual student, or one form you can use for the whole class. Use either of these forms to note any observations you make of students throughout the course of the school day. On page 37 you will find an example of an individual anecdotal record form.

The difficulty in using the form in a binder method is that it is disruptive and indiscreet. It takes several seconds, if not minutes, for you to locate the binder (usually at your desk in the back of the room), find the page for the individual student, and then record what you observed. In the time that it has taken you to do this, your lesson has become disrupted. This makes the binder inconvenient to use. Also, making notes in the binder is not very discreet. Students will quickly determine what it is you are doing when you scurry to your desk and write something down. You may wish to choose a method that will be more discreet.

Anecdotal records are carefully documented notes of certain events, behaviors, and skills.

Another way to go about recording your anecdotal notes is by using sticky notes, or mailing labels. With sticky notes you can quickly pull them out of your pocket, jot down your observation, then discreetly place the note pad back in your pocket. At the end of the school day, after students have left, you can take the time to place the note on a student page in a notebook.

Mailing labels work the same way but have an added management benefit. If you take the time to print or type your students' names on the top corner of each mailing label you can then make multiple copies of this list with mailing label sheets that can be used in the copy machine. Then, as you observe a student, you can write the note on his/her mailing label. This label is then placed on the student's page in your notebook at a convenient time. The management benefit is that at a glance you can see which students you have not yet observed by looking at which labels are still on the mailing label sheet. Without a system that enables you to know at a glance who has not yet been observed, inevitably there will be students that you never observe. We are naturally drawn to students that are having problems academically or behaviorally. Average students tend to receive less attention. With this management method, you can be assured that you have observed each of your students.

One final suggestion might be to use index cards to record your anecdotal notes. These cards can then be filed under each student's name in a file card box. If you take the time to print each student's name on the top of the index cards you can be assured that each child has been observed during a specified time period, just like with the mailing label system. The file cards can be as discreet as the sticky notes because you can keep them in your pocket and take them out only as needed. They can be filed in the file box later that day, or after school when the students are not present.

Regardless of what anecdotal system you ultimately decide to use, the important step is the review and analysis of the notes collected. Once you have collected all your "objective" anecdotal notes, you must interpret what you have observed. Look for themes or trends in that child's behavior, or academic skills. Your analysis of the notes may result in something as simple as changing the seat of a particular student, or something more serious such as an instructional program addition or change. If your notes do not give you a complete picture of the student, think about what you should observe in the future to help you better understand that student.

> We are naturally drawn to students that are having problems academically or behaviorally. Average students tend to receive less attention.

Individual Student
Anecdotal Record Form

Student's Name: _____

Date	Observation:	Watch for:

Reprinted from TCM781 Language Arts Assessment, *Teacher Created Materials, 1994*

Checklists

Checklists are lists of skills or behaviors to be checked off by the observer as a simple "yes-no" rating. The check indicates whether or not the skill or behavior was present. With the checklist there is no need to judge how well the skills are performed, only that they are present. The checklist is very useful to teachers because they can help keep observations focused. Also, checklists are extremely easy, fast, and convenient to use.

Making a Checklist

Constructing a checklist helps us consider our priorities and goals for students. It also helps put us in the frame of mind to become better kidwatchers (Goodman, Bird, & Goodman, 1992). In order to make a skills checklist, you need to do a task analysis to find out what goes into the achievement of a particular end. For example, if you wanted to make a checklist for reading, you would first have to define what reading is and what effective readers do. This can be a very time consuming process. A less time intensive way to acquire the list of items to include on a checklist would be to consult your teacher's manual scope and sequence chart, your district or state framework, or you may purchase a checklist that has already been prepared for your grade level.

Once you have identified the skills you want to observe, you need to decide how often you want to observe them. Most commonly teachers hope to observe each skill once each quarter. You should design your checklist with enough spaces to accommodate the frequency of observations you hope to make. A sample language arts quarterly checklist for grades 1-2 can be found on the next four pages.

Concluding Remarks

We have always observed our students making mental notes about academic progress and behavior. The anecdotal record process merely requires that we make written notes of these observations so they can be analyzed after several notes are collected. Several methods for managing anecdotal records were suggested making the recording process less time consuming and frustrating.

Checklists of skills can also be used when observing students. Checklists are easy to mark because you are not judging how well the skills are performed, only that they are present.

> With the checklist there is no need to judge how well the skills are performed, only that they are present.

38

Language Arts Development Checklist

Student's Name _____ Grade _____

Rating Scale   1 = Rarely Observed
                     2 = Occasionally Observed
                     3 = Often Observed

Skill	Quarter			
Oral Language Development	1	2	3	4
Expresses ideas orally with fluency				
Participates in conversation				
Takes turns in conversation				
Participates in small group discussions				
Participates in large group discussions				
Role plays				
Gives directions				
Uses expanded vocabulary				
Explains thinking				
Elaborates responses				
Listening Skills Development	1	2	3	4
Listens attentively:				
in one to one interactions				
in small group discussions				
in large group discussions				
to stories read aloud				
Can retell a story				
Comprehends verbal directions				
Recalls information accurately				
Asks questions/seeks clarification				

Reprinted from TCM773 Language Arts Assessment, *Teacher Created Materials, 1994*

39

Language Arts Development Checklist (cont.)

Skill	Quarter			
Reading Development	**1**	**2**	**3**	**4**
Knows letter names				
Knows letter sounds				
Understands directionality:				
top to bottom				
left to right				
turns pages in order				
One to one correspondence (finger/word)				
Has basic sight vocabulary				
Uses picture cues				
Uses context to identify meaning				
Makes meaningful substitutions				
Recognizes language patterns				
Monitors reading and self-corrects				
Makes and confirms predictions				
Selects appropriate reading material				
Reads a variety of materials				
Checks books out of school library				
Checks books out of public library				
Literature Response	**1**	**2**	**3**	**4**
Retells story				
Summarizes story				
Sequences story events accurately				
Relates reading to personal experience				
Awareness of story elements:				
setting				
characters				
Discusses story with others				
Gives opinion about the story				
Extends reading through related projects				

Reprinted from TCM773 Language Arts Assessment, *Teacher Created Materials, 1994*

Language Arts Development Checklist (cont.)

Skill	Quarter			
Work Patterns	1	2	3	4
Begins works promptly				
Stays on task				
Shows organization				
Self-directed				
Self-motivated				
Takes risks as a learner				
Works effectively with others				
Is able to self-evaluate				
Spelling	1	2	3	4
Uses random letters				
Uses invented spelling:				
initial consonant present				
initial and final consonant present				
some vowels present				
Invented spelling makes sense				
High frequency words spelled correctly				
Writing Mechanics	1	2	3	4
Prints letters horizontally on page				
Leaves spaces between words				
Uses age appropriate handwriting				
Uses capital letters:				
for names				
"I"				
at the beginning of a sentence				
Uses correct punctuation				
periods				
question marks				
exclamation points				
Writes in complete sentences				

Reprinted from TCM773 Language Arts Assessment, *Teacher Created Materials, 1994*

Language Arts Development Checklist (cont.)

Skill	Quarter			
Writing	**1**	**2**	**3**	**4**
Writes 1-5 sentence stories				
Writes 6-10 sentence stories				
Writes 11-20 sentence stories				
Stories have a beginning/middle/end				
Stories develop sequentially				
Uses descriptive words				
Uses story elements:				
setting				
character				
Engages promptly in writing task				
Sustains attention to writing task				
Self-selects writing topics				
Shares and discusses writing				
Revises for clarity				
Other	**1**	**2**	**3**	**4**

Reprinted from TCM773 Language Arts Assessment, Teacher Created Materials, 1994

Involving Students and
Parents in Assessment

Partners in Learning

Teachers across the country are seeing learning as a joint venture
between themselves and students. Naturally, then, the responsibility for evaluation should also be shared between teachers and students. Self-evaluation makes the students aware of their own learning, their progress, and their growth throughout the school year.
Additionally, involving students in decision making regarding their
own evaluation puts them in a position of power where their own
future is concerned. Self-evaluation challenges students to be
thoughtful judges of their own work, thereby making them key play-
ers in the assessment process. Student self-evaluation is an indis-
pensable part of any learning and assessment program that strives to
have students take responsibility for their own learning.

Beyond trying to keep students involved, we also take great pains to
keep parents informed regarding student progress and classroom
activities. Recently, however, teachers are going beyond mere dis-
tribution of information. Parents are now being invited to take part
in evaluating their child's growth and progress. If parents take a
more active role in assessment, they will naturally become more

> Self-evaluation chal-
> lenges students to be
> thoughtful judges of
> their own work, there-
> by making them key
> players in the process of
> assessment.

involved in their child's schoolwork. Another benefit of parent evaluation is clearly seen at parent conference time. Parents will be more informed and, therefore, better able to discuss their child's progress with you. Now the conference becomes a two-way conversation between teacher and parent rather than a one-way monologue performed by the teacher and directed at the parent. Involving parents completes the assessment cycle because all three participants in the child's education, the teacher, the child, and the parent, are included.

Student Self-Reflection

By taking time to reflect, students can determine where their strengths, weaknesses, and interests lie.

Self-evaluation requires reflection about both academic work and attitude. Perhaps difficulty with social studies concepts has little to do with content, and rather everything to do with motivation. By taking the time to reflect, students can determine where their strengths, and weaknesses, and interests lie. This self-evaluation process can also help students to understand that they are ultimately responsible for their own learning.

Student reflection is a major component of student self-evaluation. You can begin this reflection process slowly by asking students to reflect on one particular sample of work. Or, if you feel your students are ready, you can have them reflect on their growth and progress on work over time, particularly if you are using portfolios. When reflecting on just one assignment, the student becomes aware of how well directions were followed and standards were met. Reflections of work over time require a deeper look at growth and progress. Either of these reflections can be prompted by forms or generated as free flowing essays. A sample student self-reflection form can be found on the next page.

Although reflections are typically thought to be for the older student, it is also possible for primary students to participate. You can introduce younger students to the reflection process by encouraging them to reflect orally while you record their thoughts in writing. They can be prompted by asking what they like about their work.

We cannot expect students to jump right into self-evaluation. Traditionally students do classroom work, then wait for the teacher to return it with a grade on top. Evaluating your own work is not easy and taking responsibility for it is certainly a challenge. It will take a while for students to trust their own judgments, so be patient.

Writing Reflections

Name _____

Date _____

1. After reading my story I feel...

   _____

   _____

2. I have improved in:

   _____   writing complete sentences
   _____   using capital letters
   _____   using corroct punctuation
   _____   spelling
   _____   telling a story
   _____   using descriptive language
   _____   handwriting

3. I am most proud of:

   _____

   _____

4. Next time I write I will try to:

   _____

   _____

Reprinted from TCM777 Language Arts Assessment, *Teacher Created Materials, 1994*

Parent Perspectives

Traditionally, parents have been left out of the assessment process. This is unfortunate because parents are in a unique position to provide teachers with certain information that would otherwise be inaccessible. You might wish to ask the parent to monitor certain behaviors and attitudes at home that can affect school performance. When we give parents the opportunity to assess their child's learning, they become more aware of what to observe and how their child learns (Hill & Ruptic, 1994). If parents are involved in their child's evaluation on a continual basis, they will be better prepared to discuss their child's progress with you. Parents are now in a position to offer information rather than just receive it (Anthony, Johnson, Mickelson, & Preece, 1991).

> If parents are involved in their child's evaluation on a continual basis, they will be better prepared to discuss the child's progress with you.

By involving parents in the assessment process, they will better understand their child's strengths and areas that need improvement. Having this valuable knowledge can enable parents to become more involved in helping their child succeed in school. By making parents our partners, we can work collaboratively to help the child do as well as possible. You can get parents involved in their child's education by asking them to complete surveys, questionnaires, and observation forms.

Teacher/Student Conferences

The conference between teacher and student can serve two purposes: to review growth and progress and to plan the next step in the instructional program. If you are using portfolios in your classroom, this process will be easier and more efficient. A glance through the accumulated work gives both teacher and student a good idea of how the student is progressing, what has been accomplished, and what should come next (Jasmine, 1993). The student should be every bit as involved in this conference as you are. Try to ask open ended questions in order to encourage the student to do most of the talking. Some sample questions are listed below. You should also encourage the student to take this opportunity to ask you questions as well.

- ◆ What have you been reading?
- ◆ Tell me about the story you have been reading.
- ◆ What have you written?
- ◆ What have you worked to improve in your writing?
- ◆ How do you feel about your progress?
- ◆ What do you want to achieve by our next conference?

The most difficult aspect of conferencing with students is finding the time to do it. If you schedule your time so that you do one conference a day, everyday, you will have more than enough time to conference with every student each quarter. The conference should be brief and only last about ten minutes or so. They may take a little longer at first as students learn the conference process. However, in time, they should move along quite smoothly. The time you take to conference with students will be well spent.

Teacher/Parent Conferences

If parents have participated in the evaluation process of their child, then the teacher/parent conference can be a two-way exchange. In fact, if you are using portfolios in your classroom and sending them home on a regular basis, parents should be able to offer considerable input during the conference. The key is to work along with the parent collaboratively in discussing progress and making plans for the future. Parents, however, may not be accustomed to this type of conference approach. It will be up to you to create a situation for parents that is comfortable and non-threatening. You may also want to send the parent a list of topics you would like to discuss at the conference a week prior to your meeting. The parent will then feel prepared to discuss their child with you.

The key is to work along with the parent collaboratively in discussing progress and making plans for the future.

Student/Parent Conferences

Now that we are asking students to take part in evaluating their progress, we should also allow them to take part in sharing it. Students can be given the opportunity to participate in the conference or lead the conference with their parents. Younger students can attend the conference and choose one item from the portfolio to tell their parent about. It is like a "show and tell" of progress made. Older students can lead the entire conference showing parents several examples of their best work, as well as, their plans for improvement in the future. At first it will probably be necessary for you to attend the entire conference with the child and parent. However, when working with older students who are properly trained and have become accustomed to leading a conference, you can take a back seat in the process. In fact, you can schedule several of these conferences at a time and simply "rove" around the classroom listening and observing.

To prepare students for leading the student/parent conference you might ask them to brainstorm a list of the work they would like to share with their parent. This is another instance where having portfolios in your classroom can really be beneficial and efficient. After students have selected their samples, they can script or outline how they would like to present it to their parents if they wish. You may need to offer guidance and suggestions here, or perhaps the class can brainstorm ideas together. Once students have a good idea of what they are going to say, they should work with a partner and practice. The final step is for students to create an invitation for the conference to present to their parents. If parents are not accustomed to having a conference with their child, you may want to send home a letter along with the invitation describing the process. Or, if you have the time, schedule an after school parent meeting to explain the purpose and procedure of the student/parent conference.

Once the student/parent conference is complete, you may want all parties to reflect on the experience in writing. This way if you did not attend the entire conference, you can get a feel for what transpired, and also any concerns or clarifications that might have to be made.

Students should be invited to participate in the assessment process as much as possible.

Concluding Remarks

Students should be invited to participate in the assessment process as much as possible. They can complete self-reflections in order to help them think critically about their own growth and progress. They can also be invited to participate in a teacher/student conference with you. The discussion during this conference should involve both you and the student, rather than you talking "at" the student. The more ownership they take of the assessment process the better they will understand their achievements and weaknesses.

Students can also be invited to conference with parents. Proudly displaying their best work to mom and dad can be a significant event in the child's life. The parent also feels more involved and informed if both the teacher and the student can comment on progress.

Authentic Assessment for Language Arts

Background Information

Recently there has been a revolution in the way we teach language arts. We no longer view reading and writing as isolated tasks to be constantly drilled and tested. Reading and writing are now taught in conjunction with each other and integrated throughout all subject areas. This whole language approach to language arts instruction focuses on literacy development and is not as concerned with product as it is with process.

As our focus changes from isolated skills to an integrated whole language approach, it becomes necessary to reevaluate our tools of assessment. Do basal reading tests and multiple choice writing tests really measure reading and writing aptitude? Essentially what these tests measure is the student's forced response to isolated, disconnected questions. In order to get a more complete picture of the reader and writer, a more authentic means of assessment is necessary. For reading, miscue analysis can provide a wealth of information about the proficiency of a reader. In writing, conferences are now being used widely for assessment of writing skills.

> As our focus changes from isolated skills to an integrated whole language approach, it becomes necessary to reevaluate our tools of assessment.

Miscue Analysis

Miscue Analysis is a type of reading assessment that considers both the reading of the text and the retelling of the story as equally important. In the past we have determined a child's reading ability based on how well he or she read out loud, regardless of comprehension. Miscue analysis takes reading assessment to a much higher level, a level more consistent with the whole language philosophy. It is therefore no surprise that Ken Goodman, often noted as the father of whole language, developed the miscue analysis procedure. Goodman didn't think reading ability could be assessed based on paper and pencil tests. Instead he developed the miscue analysis procedure wherein students read out loud and then tell what they remember about the story. This procedure grew from Goodman's research, begun over three decades ago, working with real kids reading real books in real schools.

Miscue analysis is based on the notion that every reading response is a result of the reader's knowledge of language, experiences, and the printed text.

Goodman defines a miscue as an unexpected response by a reader to the printed text, in other words a "mistake." If we can understand how the miscue relates to the expected response we can begin to understand how the child is using the reading process (Goodman, 1982). The miscue, therefore, provides a window into the strategies and cueing systems (semantic, syntactic, and grapho-phonic, and pragmatic) the child uses when reading an unknown text. Miscue analysis is based on the notion that every reading response is a result of the reader's knowledge of language, experiences, and the printed text. By analyzing the miscues, you can determine the student's confirming and predicting reading skills as well as his/her control of the cueing systems. Control of all four cueing systems leads to effective meaning construction and comprehension.

Reading Cueing Systems

There are four cueing systems a reader uses when constructing meaning from text: the semantic system, the syntactic system, the grapho-phonic system, and the pragmatic system (Perkins, 1993). The semantic cueing system refers to the way language is used and the words chosen to convey meaning. The semantic system gives language its life. It has to do with the way in which we express meaning, sense, ideas, and thought (Weaver, 1988). This system relies heavily on context clues for word identification. In the syntactic cueing system, the reader uses knowledge of language patterns and grammatical structure to identify unknown words. This system is the frame that supports meaning. The grapho-phonic cueing system is based on letter-sound relationships. This system is visually expressed. In other words, it's the black marks on the page. When relying on this system, students typically sound out words they do not know. The pragmatic cueing system refers to the practical use of language. Proficient readers use all four cueing systems simultaneously in order to construct meaning. Miscue analysis helps us determine which cueing systems the child uses when reading and if there is an over-emphasis on the grapho-phonic cueing system.

Miscue Analysis Procedure

The first step in the miscue process is to select a book for the child to read that is unfamiliar to him or her, and would be considered slightly challenging. Goodman (1982) suggests that it is necessary to have at least 25 miscues in the reading in order to do a complete analysis. If you are a miscue novice, it may be easier for you to have a few books that you use regularly when doing miscue analysis because it helps to be very familiar with the book. The child must be given the entire text, complete with the illustrations. Anything less would not provide the child with the proper context in which to attempt to construct meaning of the text.   Picture books are now available with very sophisticated vocabulary to use with older students. However, if you wish to use a novel instead, make sure the child reads the first chapter for the miscue analysis. If you were to select any other chapter in the unfamiliar book, the child may not have the necessary background information to construct meaning.

The child must be given the entire text, complete with the illustrations. Anything less would not provide the child with the proper context in which to attempt to construct meaning of the text and is therefore not fair to the reader.

In order to do a miscue analysis, you will need a photocopy of the entire text the student is reading, with several spaces between lines so that you can write the miscues in as the child reads. You can use a basic marking system such as the example on the following page, or simply use a marking system that you are personally comfortable with.   The marking system on page 52 is very basic.   Yetta Goodman, Dorothy Watson, and Carolyn Burke (1987) describe a more sophisticated system in their book *Reading Miscue Inventory: Alternative Procedures*. Whatever marking system you choose, the procedure is to note the miscues as the child is reading the text to you by listening carefully to the reading. You may elect to tape record the child's reading if you are worried that you may not be able to catch everything as the child reads. This is a fairly common practice when doing miscue analysis. While the child is reading you should not offer assistance. If you supply unknown words or correct miscues the valuable information this procedure can provide will likely not come to light (Harp, 1993). It is suggested that you inform students that you will not be available for assistance prior to beginning the miscue procedure. Suggest to students that they guess or skip words that are unfamiliar. An example of a marked text can be found on page 53.

Marking System

Substitutions: written directly above the expected
                  response

Omissions: circle the word that is omitted

Insertions: indicate the insertion in the appropriate
                  place in the text with a caret (^) and note
                  what word was substituted

Repeated Words: shown by drawing a line under the word
                  the number of times the child repeats the
                  word

After the child has finished reading and all miscues are recorded, you can begin the retelling portion of the miscue analysis. In this part of the miscue procedure, you simply ask the student to retell the story. The retelling is the most important aspect of the miscue analysis because the focus of this procedure is on whether or not the child is able to comprehend the text. It is important to remember that during the retelling you should never interrupt. Only offer coaching to try to get more information from the child. Statements such as "Can you tell me more about..." or "Can you explain...." are good coaching questions. You should make notes during the retelling or tape record the session for later review. After the retelling, you can categorize and analyze the miscues as well as statements made by the student during the retelling. Detailed information about analyzing the miscues is on page 54. When analyzing the retelling statements, ask yourself if the child was able to capture the essential meaning of the story or text. Comprehension is the goal of reading. If the child reads the story without a single miscue, yet is unable to tell you anything about what is read, the reading is totally meaningless. You may find it easier to analyze the retelling if you categorize statements made by the student. Retelling categories may include: character statements, setting statements, plot statements, theme statements, and misconceptions.

Comprehension is the goal of reading. If the child reads the story without a single miscue, yet is unable to tell you anything about what is read, the reading is totally meaningless.

Ask any coyote near the ~~Pecos~~ _Peak_ River in western Texas who was the best cowboy who ever lived. He will answer Pecos Bill. When Pecos Bill was a baby he was as ~~tough~~ _rough_ as a pine (knot) His best friends were _all_ grizzly bears. Pecos Bill could have grown up just fine in Texas. But one day his ~~pappy~~ _daddy_ decided to move because people were moving in fifty miles away. He thought it was getting too crowded!

Analyzing Miscues

You can use a basic four step approach to analyzing miscues. The first step is to count the total number of miscues. Then, count miscues that are acceptable substitutions. Finally, count miscues that were originally unacceptable but were successfully corrected. Add the totals of acceptable and corrected miscues counted. The sum is the number of miscues that are semantically acceptable. Compute this sum as a percentage of the total number of miscues. In general, proficient readers usually produce miscues that are semantically and syntactically acceptable at least 70 percent of the time (Weaver, 1988). This final score can be considered the "comprehending" score. It expresses the reader's ability to focus on meaning construction. Remember, the number of miscues is not as important as the effect the miscues have on the child's ability to comprehend the story.

Remember, the number of miscues is not as important as the effect the miscues have on the child's ability to comprehend the story.

In the analysis, you should look for evidence of the use of the four cueing systems. However, the most important single indication of the reader's proficiency is the semantic acceptability of his miscues before correction (Goodman, 1982). Ask yourself if the miscue was an acceptable substitution for the context. For example, substituting "afraid" for "frightened" would be an example of an appropriate semantic substitution. You should also look for syntactic similarity among substitutions. Does the student substitute a noun for a noun and a verb for a verb? To assist in your analysis of the miscues you may find the form on page 55 helpful.

Although miscue analysis is a time consuming process, there is no doubt that it provides invaluable information about the child's reading ability. Teachers say that once they have done just one miscue analysis they never again listen to students read in the same way (Harp, 1993).

Miscue Analysis Form

Student's Name_____

Age _____ Grade_____ Date _____

Title of book_____

1. Did the miscues go with the proceeding text?

   _____

2. Did the miscues go with the following text?

   _____

3. Did the miscues leave the essential meaning of the sentence intact?

   _____

4. Did the miscues leave the essential meaning of the story intact?

   _____

5. Were the miscues corrected?

   _____

6. Were the miscues appropriate substitutions?

   _____

7. Did the miscues have graphic similarity?

   _____

8. Did the miscues have sound similarity?

   _____

9. Did the miscues have grammatical similarity?

   _____

10. Are the miscues grammatically sensible?

   _____

Other Observations:

Reprinted from TCM777 Language Arts Assessment, *Teacher Created Materials, 1994*

Writing Conferences

A major component of the writing process has become the writing conference. In the writing conference the student writer reads the story and then talks with either a peer or the teacher about what he/she has written. Then the peer or teacher responds to the piece, offering comments and suggestions to the writer for future drafts. These comments are made orally to the student, as well as in writing on a conference form. Having the opportunity to talk about their writing with others gives the author a better sense of audience and clarity of the writing. The writing conference process is described in detail below.

Parents are frequently eager to assist in the classroom and the writing conference provides them with a vital role.

Some teachers avoid writing conferences because they don't know how to find time in their hectic schedules to meet with students. However, there are several options available for writing respondents. Older students should be able to conference with each other in addition to conferencing with you. These older students can also be used to conference with students in primary grades. If your own time is limited, you may wish to solicit parent volunteers. Parents are frequently eager to assist in the classroom and the writing conference provides them with a vital role. It is important, however, that you take the time to train parents on the conference process. Perhaps this can be arranged as an after school meeting or "training session." At this parent meeting you could not only describe the writing conference process, but also hold a mock writing conference so parents can see the process in action. The minimal time you spend arranging a training session will pay off in the long run as parents become self-directed during conference time.

Conducting Writing Conferences

You should try to schedule a writing workshop time several days during the week when writing conferences can take place. Having a regular schedule will help establish a routine with students, as well as helping you to make arrangements for parent or older student volunteers (Calkins, 1994). Because only several students will be conferencing at any one time, you will need to plan activities for the other students. Perhaps you can direct the rest of the class while the parents conference with individual students. Or you can assign a self-directed activity for the class while you conference with individuals. If you arrange for yourself to be free for conferences, yet feel the parents are capable of leading the conferences themselves, you may want to circulate among the conferences as they are in progress.

There are many ways to structure writing conferences. One common way to structure the conference is described in steps below.

1. The first step of the conference is to allow the writer to read the piece on his/her own. The writer should not be interrupted during the reading. While the writer reads the piece, make mental notes regarding correction of miscues.

2. Following this reading, the writer should be allowed to talk about the piece or ask questions. For example, suggest to the parent or peer that they encourage the student through coaching to answer their own questions about the writing. Suggest that the writer guess how to spell something before simply giving the answer.

3. After the writer has had ample time to discuss the writing, the respondent can begin to ask questions for clarification.

4. Finally, respondents can offer comments and suggestions to the writer to assist in the revision process.

5. Remind the students and parents to keep the conference on a positive note as much as possible!

When you conduct the conference, you have the option of writing a narrative report regarding your assessment of the writing, or you can have a form to fill in for each student immediately following the conference.

Although the writing conference is done orally, you may want some written record of what was discussed. When students or parents conduct the conference, they can make a few notes to you about the strengths of the writer's piece and any suggestions that were made. When you conduct the conference, you have the option of writing a narrative report regarding your assessment of the writing, or you can have a form to fill in for each student following the conference. An example of a conference form for a student-teacher writing conference has been included on page 58.

Concluding Remarks

When we use a whole language approach to reading and writing instruction in our classrooms, we are forced to examine traditional methods of assessment for these content areas. In order to truly assess reading and writing ability we must allow students to actually read and write. Miscue analysis is an authentic method of assessment for reading in which we observe a child reading and then analyze the miscues. Writing conferences allow students to talk about their original writing with other students and parents, as well as the teacher.

Student-Teacher Writing Conference

Student's Name _____ Date _____

1. What is the student's attitude toward the piece?
   _____
   _____

2. What is the student's reaction when he/she sees or hears a miscue in the story?
   _____
   _____

3. Do miscues reveal signs of growth such as movement toward convention?
   _____
   _____

4. Does the student ask questions about conventions?
   _____
   _____

5. Does the student revise or correct during language use?
   _____
   _____

6. What types of changes does the student make when revising or self-correcting?
   _____
   _____

Additional Comments:
_____
_____
_____
_____

Reprinted from TCM777 Language Arts Assessment, *Teacher Created Materials, 1994*

Authentic Assessment for Mathematics

Background Information

Traditionally we have assessed mathematics ability based on the number of correct answers on a page full of computational problems. Learning and memorizing facts, therefore, was the key component to the mathematics instructional program. Recently, however, many teachers have started placing a greater emphasis on mathematical understanding, problem-solving, hands-on experiences, and collaborative work. This change in the instructional program can be attributed to well-informed teachers and the work of the National Council of Teachers of Mathematics (NCTM). In their *Curriculum and Evaluation Standards for School Mathematics* (National Council of Teachers of Mathematics, 1989) it is stated that teachers should realize that their students will be using mathematics in a world where calculators, computers, and other forms of technology are readily available. Therefore, application of mathematics, rather than mere fact acquisition, is what will be expected of them in the workplace and in life, and consequently mathematics instruction should mirror this real life application. As our mathematics instruction changes, we must also change mathematics assessment. Multiple choice tests that simply require students to add, subtract, multiply, and divide numbers are no longer sufficient.

> **Recently, however, many teachers have started placing a greater emphasis on mathematical understanding, problem solving, hands-on experiences, and collaborative work.**

To make students actively involved in the mathematics classroom it is necessary to take an inquiry-oriented approach. Problem solving becomes a medium for doing and learning mathematics that pervades instruction (Webb, 1993). Along with this new active role for students comes a new role for teachers. Teachers in inquiry-oriented classroom situations change from traditional instructor as the dispenser of knowledge to the guide or facilitator of instructional experiences (Webb, 1993). The teacher's job is to help students construct meaning and understanding. Assessment is an important tool in determining the meanings students are assigning to mathematical ideas. While portfolios and observation-based assessment can certainly be used for mathematics assessment, two types of authentic assessment unique to mathematics are described below: enhanced multiple choice questions and open-ended tasks.

Types of Authentic Math Assessments

Two new types of authentic math assessments include enhanced multiple choice questions and open-ended tasks. They are gaining popularity as schools across the country adopt the mathematical goals defined by the National Council of Teachers of Mathematics. In their document *Curriculum and Evaluation Standards for School Mathematics* (1989) the Council defines five general goals for all students in mathematics. The goals are (1) that students learn to value mathematics, (2) that students become confident in their ability to do mathematics, (3) that students become mathematical problem solvers, (4) that students learn to communicate mathematically, and (5) that students learn to reason mathematically. Basic drill and kill of simple computation problems will never prepare students to meet these goals. Consequently, enhanced multiple choice questions and open-ended tasks were developed as a more authentic means of instruction and assessment. It is important that both of these assessments are integrated into the instructional program. In this way, the learning tasks have the same character as the assessment tasks When writing the authentic assessment task, you should include the following characteristics: (1) the task can be solved in a number of ways, (2) the task elicits a range of responses, (3) the task requires students to communicate in some way, and (4) the task stimulates the best possible performance of the student. If assessment tasks are a culmination of learning, they should pose problems that require students to synthesize what they have learned (Cooney, Badger, & Wilson, 1993).

Enhanced Multiple Choice Questions

Enhanced multiple choice assessments ask students to employ several concepts in order to arrive at a correct answer. Unlike traditional multiple choice questions that can have only one right answer, enhanced multiple choice questions can have more than one right answer. For example, the enhanced multiple choice sample problem #1 on the following page can have two right answers: 4 and 5, or 3 and 6. Sample problem #2 can also have two right answers: 6 and 2, or 5 and 1. Compare these enhanced multiple choice problems to traditional math problems such as the one below.

$$5 + 4 = \underline{\quad}$$

The enhanced multiple choice problems require critical thinking and problem solving strategies in order to arrive at the answer. The traditional problem merely requires rote memorization. Inherent to the enhanced multiple choice problem is the requirement that students use more than one mathematical strategy to solve the problem. Typically, because of their complexity, enhanced multiple choice questions take two to three minutes to solve.

Inherent to the enhanced multiple choice problem is the requirement that students use more than one mathematical strategy to solve the problem.

Although enhanced multiple choice questions require a higher level of thinking than ordinary multiple choice questions, they are still quick and easy to correct because there is a limited number of correct answers. If you want to challenge students you might require them to explain how they arrived at their answer. Now, students are incorporating writing into mathematics and working toward the NCTM goal of being able to communicate mathematically.

Two enhanced multiple choice question samples can be found on the next page. Both samples are very basic. However, as suggested above, students can be asked to explain how they arrived at the answer.

Sample 1

Addition (using up to 6), with
fixed sum

$$\square + \square = 9$$

Choose two numbers from

to form a problem with the sum of 9.

Sample 2

Subtraction (using up to 6), with
fixed difference

$$\square - \square = 4$$

Choose two numbers from

1 2 3 4 5 6

to form a difference of 4.

Reprinted from TCM770 Math Assessment, *Teacher Created Materials, 1994*

Open-Ended Tasks

An open-ended task presents students with a description of a problem situation, and poses a mathematical question for students to respond to in writing or by drawing. The question should be designed to find out how well the students can think, solve, and communicate about the given situation (California State Department of Education, 1991). The problem must be open-ended enough to allow for more than one right answer. Open-ended tasks can take anywhere from 15 minutes to up to two weeks to solve. In some cases, students can be allowed to use calculators, manipulatives, or computers to assist them in solving the open-ended task.

When writing an open-ended task, try to create an interesting situation for students. This will initially get their interest in the question. Also, be sure the question allows for multiple solutions. On the next page you will find an example of an open-ended task. Notice the situation involves purchasing a snack at school, an interesting situation that students can relate to. Also notice that there are several correct answers for this task, and the response requires writing. Answers to open-ended tasks are scored using a rubric that is clearly defined and discussed prior to students' engagement in the task. For more detailed information on rubrics, see chapter 4.

Classroom Structure

How you use enhanced multiple choice questions and open-ended tasks in your classroom is up to you and depends on your assessment purpose, classroom population, and management style. Several options are available. You can use the questions with the whole class while modeling strategies on the overhead projector, or students can do the problems on their own. Another option is to have students work on the problems in small groups. This method gives you time to circulate in the class and observe students as they cooperatively solve the problem. Keep in mind, however, that these types of assessment problems require far more time than their traditional counterparts. Be sure students are given an adequate amount of time to work with the problem be that ten minutes, or ten days.

Concluding Remarks

As more and more schools adopt the NCTM standards for mathematics, assessment methods will change. Enhanced multiple choice questions and open-ended tasks require students to apply mathematics rather than just compute numbers. With the renewed emphasis on being able to think mathematically in the real world, these new assessments will be excellent preparations for the students' futures.

> How you use enhanced multiple choice questions and open-ended tasks in your classroom is up to you and depends on your assessment purpose, classroom population, and management style.

63

Sample Open-Ended Task

Situation: Raphael just moved to the United States from Mexico. Your teacher asks you to take Raphael out at recess time and show him the snack vending machines. Raphael is delighted to know that he can purchase a snack each day. However, he doesn't understand American money. The snack machine accepts exact change only, so Raphael asks you to give him the possible combinations of coins that can be used to pay for any of the 60-cent snacks.

The Task: Design a reference sheet for Raphael that will show him the coin combinations he can use for the snack machine. Then, explain in writing how you developed the reference sheet.

Your Response:

Authentic Assessment
for Science

Background Information

Traditionally, science has been taught as an accumulation of factual knowledge sometimes linked thematically and taught with enthusiasm, sometimes used only to fill some empty time at the end of the day. Science is much more than the study of facts and acquisition of scientific knowledge. It involves observing, predicting, testing, predicting, and discovering what certain results might mean. Students can achieve a better understanding of scientific concepts if they are allowed and encouraged to actively participate in the scientific process. This can be accomplished through hands-on investigations that require students to perform an experiment using the scientific process.

Students can achieve a better understanding of scientific concepts if they are allowed and encouraged to actively participate in the scientific process.

Hands-On Investigations

In order for students to truly understand scientific concepts, we must provide an activity-based approach to the science curriculum. This goal can be met by allowing students to participate in hands-on scientific investigations that require students to put the scientific process into practice in order to answer a scientific question. Investigations and assessments are very tightly linked. In the course of investigating, students will be exploring subject matter using thinking skills. The skills themselves are hard to separate. So, in many cases the investigation is the assessment.

There are several decisions to make prior to creating the investigation. You must choose the subject matter to be investigated, decide which process skills to target, determine the way in which students will report the results of their investigation, and of course, create a rubric or checklist to assess their science investigation skills. The subject matter of the investigation is based on the unit of study or science theme. Some suggestions for science themes could be energy, plants, patterns of change, ecology, life cycles, and systems and interactions. Once you have chosen the subject matter, you should choose the process skills that compliment that subject. There are six key process skills including observing, communicating, classifying, inferring, relating, and applying. Other process skills can also be included such as describing, predicting, concluding, interpreting, and comparing.

The subject matter of the investigation is based on the unit of study or science theme.

For assessment purposes, you must now decide if you want to create a simple checklist of process skills to use when observing students during the investigation, or if you want to create a rubric to assess the investigation results. After you have made these important decisions, you can create the investigation. An example of an investigation can be found on page 67. The sample investigation asks students to observe leaves using their senses. Once you have created the investigation, you will need to create a data capture sheet for students to record their results. This can be in written form, or you may choose to have students draw picture representations. An example of a data capture sheet for the leaves investigation can be found on page 68. The data capture sheet is scored using the rubric you create for the investigation.

Concluding Remarks

Science is not a subject that should be taught by having students read a text and answer questions. If we want students to understand the scientific process, we must allow them to practice it by doing actual hands-on investigations. It is only when students are allowed to be actively involved in science instruction that they will truly come to understand the steps of the scientific process.

Leaves: An Investigation

Relevant Skills:

Observing/Communicating

Knowledge Base:

Is familiar with the function of the five senses

Setting Up the Investigation

This investigation would be appropriate at any time of the year except winter in most parts of the northern hemisphere. (It would be interesting to investigate leaves in the fall and then repeat the investigation in the spring to compare the differences in the leaves that could be observed.)

- Bring in branches from trees and bushes with different kinds of leaves and display them around the classroom, allowing students to become familiar with them and discuss them.

- If possible, take a nature walk and allow students to collect leaves.

- Tell students they will be investigating leaves and then sharing what they find out.

- Encourage students to discuss the leaves that people eat or use for flavoring, but caution them that they will not be able to taste the leaves during this investigation, since some leaves could be dangerous to eat.

- Have each child choose two leaves to observe. Give them the "Leaves Response Sheet" to complete. Allow plenty of time.

Reprinted from TCM771 Science Assessment, *Teacher Created Materials, 1994*

Leaves Data Capture Sheet

Name _____Date _____

Lay one leaf in each box. If your leaves are too big, draw them.

Leaf #1

Leaf #2

Look at Leaf #1.
What do you see?
_____
_____

Look at Leaf #2.
What do you see?
_____
_____

Listen to Leaf #1.
What do you hear?
_____
_____

Listen to Leaf #2.
What do you hear?
_____
_____

Put your nose near Leaf #1.
What do you smell?
_____
_____

Put your nose near Leaf #2.
What do you smell?
_____
_____

Rub your finger over Leaf #1.
What do you feel?
_____
_____

Rub your finger over Leaf #2.
What do you feel?
_____
_____

Reprinted from TCM771 Science Assessment, *Teacher Created Materials, 1994*

Authentic Assessment for Social Studies

Background Information

It has already been asserted that learning and assessment need to compliment each other. This is particularly important where social studies is concerned. As we increase the emphasis on cooperative learning and writing during unit studies, it makes less sense to complete the unit by administering a multiple choice exam. If students write during their study, then writing should be part of their assessment. Using open-ended essays as a social studies assessment gives students an opportunity to display their knowledge using their writing skills. If students work cooperatively during their study, then part of their assessment should include a cooperative task. To assess academic as well as social skills needed for collaboration, cooperative investigations are useful. Cooperative investigations require students to work with other members of the class to solve a problem.

As more teachers move away from a social studies curriculum that merely requires students to regurgitate facts and dates, our assessment tasks also needs to ask more of students. With both cooperative investigations and open-ended essays, students are given the opportunity to show what they know by applying their knowledge and skills in meaningful, authentic contexts.

Using open-ended essays as part of social studies assessment gives students an opportunity to display their knowledge of social studies content by using their writing skills.

Cooperative Investigations

Cooperative investigations in social studies require students to work in heterogeneous groups toward a common goal of a particular task. Cooperative investigations encourage students to become partners in learning rather than competitors. Working in heterogeneous groups allows students to learn both with each other and from each other. Performing the cooperative investigation can help prepare students for individual open-ended writing assignments, the second type of social studies assessment that will be discussed in this chapter.

Organizing for Cooperative Investigations

In cooperative investigations each student has a particular job or responsibility in his/her group. Therefore, each student must make a contribution in order to successfully complete the task. It is important that each student develops the skills necessary for working with others in groups. These skills are valuable later in life as students become working adults.

You must structure the cooperative investigation so that all students have an important role in completion of the social studies related task. It is also important that groups are heterogeneously organized, not according to ability. The best group size at the primary level is two to four students, at the upper grade level the best size is between four and six students of various abilities. Groups should be gender and racially balanced as much as possible. There are five basic roles for participants in the investigation: reader, recorder, manager, leader, and monitor. The reader reads all directions and sees that they are followed. The recorder writes all group answers. The manager divides up the group work and keeps everyone on task. The leader leads discussions and keeps everyone involved. Last, the monitor watches time, hands out materials, and supplies. The roles can be adjusted based on the number of participants you decide is best. Students are assessed on the group's ability to perform the task. You may also wish to go one step further and assess their individual ability to cooperate and work effectively with a group of peers. A sample form that can be used to assess performance on the cooperative investigation follows on the next page. Notice that both social and academic objectives are included in the evaluation.

Investigation Evaluation

Cooperative Task: _____

Date _____

Number of students in the group _____

Members of the group _____
_____

1. How were decisions made? _____
   _____
   _____

2. How did students help each other achieve a common goal?
   _____
   _____

3. Did you have to intervene at any time? If so, why? _____
   _____
   _____

4. Did the group meet the cooperative investigation objective?
   Evidence or examples:
   _____
   _____
   _____
   _____

Comments on individual group members:
_____
_____
_____
_____
_____

Reprinted from TCM780 Social Studies Assessment, *Teacher Created Materials, 1994*

Open-Ended Essays

Open-ended essays ask students to apply knowledge and skills to construct an answer to the essay prompt in their own words. There can be several ways to interpret the issue or problem given to students and therefore there can be more than one answer. Students are asked to write an essay to answer the open-ended question related to the social studies unit completed.

Writing an Open-Ended Essay Prompt

The prompt for the open-ended essay includes three different parts: introduction, stimulus, and prompt. The introduction sets the stage for students to be able to respond to the prompt and may offer some necessary background information. The stimulus will vary depending on the essay question. In many instances primary sources such as quotations, passages, maps, or photographs are used. The prompt is somehow connected to the stimulus and asks an open-ended question in a brief, straightforward manner.

To write the open-ended essay prompt, consider an important issue or concept that you want to assess student's knowledge of. Then, think of the prompt you will want students to respond to in order to show their ability to apply their knowledge of the issue or concept. Make sure the question is open-ended enough to allow different interpretations by the students. Next, locate a primary source that can serve as background information or a stimulus for the prompt. Often the student's social studies book is an excellent resource for the stimulus. Then, decide how you want students to respond to the prompt. Will it be in the form of a letter, position statement, or standard essay? Finally, create a rubric to use in scoring the students' responses. A sample open-ended essay question can be found on the following page. The essays will be scored according to the rubric which is created and clearly defined prior to students' engagement in the activity.

Concluding Remarks

Rote memorization of historical dates and events will never excite students about the study of history. If we want to create interest in the subject we must change our instructional methods to include more activities that allow students to become directly involved with history. If we allow this to happen, then our assessment will have to change from multiple choice exams to cooperative investigations and open-ended essays. These two authentic forms of assessment allow students to truly show what they know about history including dates and events, but also about the people who lived at that time and their contributions.

> **To write the open-ended essay prompt, consider an important issue or concept that you want to assess student's knowledge of.**

Open-Ended Essay

Background Information:

Even before America won its independence, settlers were pushing west of the Appalachian Mountains. There was adventure and opportunity in these new lands that many could not resist. However, the trip west was no easy task. Early pioneers braved rough roads and dangerous rivers, the blistering heat of the summer and unbearable cold of the winter. Even when the pioneers found a place to settle they still struggled. The life and struggles of pioneers has been beautifully chronicled in Laura Ingalls Wilder's "Little House" Series.

An Excerpt from *The Long Winter* by Laura Ingalls Wilder (HarperCollins, 1968)

Winter has lasted so long that it seemed it would never end. It seemed that they would never really wake up. In the morning Laura got out of bed into the cold. She dressed downstairs by the fire that Pa had kindled before he went to the stable. They ate their coarse brown bread. Then all day long she and Ma and Mary ground wheat and twisted hay as fast as they could. The fire must not go out; it was very cold. They ate some coarse brown bread. Then Laura crawled into the cold bed and shivered until she grew warm enough to sleep.
Next morning she got out of bed into the cold. She dressed in the chilly kitchen by the fire. She ate her coarse brown bread. She took her turns at grounding wheat and twisting hay. But she did not ever feel awake. She felt beaten by the cold and the storms. She knew she was dull and stupid but she could not wake up.

Your Task:

You have just read a short excerpt from *The Long Winter* by Laura Ingalls Wilder. Her life as a pioneer is very different from your own life in the twentieth century. Use a concept web to help you brainstorm the ways in which your life is different from Laura's. Then, write an essay describing the ways in which your lives are different.

Reprinted from TCM780 Social Studies Assessment, *Teacher Created Materials, 1994*

Professional Organizations

Association for Supervision and Curriculum Development
1250 N. Pitt Street
Alexandria, VA 22314-1403
1-703-549-9110

International Reading Association
800 Barksdale Road
PO Box 8139
Newark, DE 19714-8139
1-800-336-READ

National Council for the Social Studies
3501 Newark Street, NW
Washington, DC 20016
1-202-966-7840

National Council of Teachers of English
1111 Kenyon Road
Urbana, IL 61801
1-800-369-6283

National Council of Teachers of Mathematics
1906 Association Drive
Reston, VA 22091-1593
1-703-620-9840

National Science Teachers Association
1840 Wilson Blvd.
Arlington, VA 22201-3000
1-800-722-NSTA

References

Anthony, R.J., Johnson, T.D., Mickelson, N.I., & Preece, A. (1991). Evaluating literacy: A perspective for change. Portsmouth, NH: Heinemann.

Barrs, M., Ellis, S., Hester, H., & Thomas, A. (1991). The primary language record. Portsmouth, NH: Heinemann.

California State Department of Education. (1991). A sampler of mathematics assessment. Sacramento, CA: Author.

California State Department of Education. (1993). California learning record. Sacramento, CA: Author.

Calkins, L.M. (1994). The art of teaching writing. Portsmouth, NH: Heinemann.

Cooney, T.J., Badger, E., & Wilson, M.R. (1993). Assessment, understanding mathematics, and distinguishing visions from mirages. In N.L. Webb & A.F. Coxford (Eds.), Assessment in the mathematics classroom (pp. 239-247). Reston, VA: National Council of Teachers of Mathematics.

Goldman, J.P. (1989, December). Student portfolios already proven in some schools. School Administrator, pp. 8-11.

Goodman, K.S. (1982). Miscues: Windows on the reading process. In F.V. Gollasch (Ed.), Language and literacy: The selected writings of Kenneth S. Goodman (pp. 93-102). Boston: Routledge & Kegan Paul.

Goodman, K.S., Bird, L.B., & Goodman, Y.M. (1992). The whole language catalog supplement on authentic assessment. New York: Macmillan.

Goodman, Y.M., Watson, D.J., & Burke, C.L. (1987). Reading miscue inventory: Alternative procedures. Katonah, NY: Richard C. Owen Publishers, Inc.

Harp, B. (Ed.). (1993). Assessment and evaluation in whole language programs. Norwood, MA: Christopher-Gordon Publishers.

Herman, J.L., Aschbacher, P.R., & Winters, L. (1992). A practical guide to alternative assessment. Alexandria, VA: Association for Supervision and Curriculum Development.

Hill, B.C., & Ruptic, C. (1994). Practical aspects of authentic assessment: Putting the pieces together. Norwood, MA: Christopher-Gordon Publishers.

Jasmine, J. (1993). Portfolios and other assessments. Westminster, CA: Teacher Created Materials.

Jasmine, J. (1994). Middle school assessment. Westminster, CA: Teacher Created Materials.

Marzano, R.J., Pickering, D., & McTighe, J. (1993). Assessing student outcomes. Alexandria, VA: Association for Supervision and Curriculum Development.

National Council of Teachers of Mathematics. (1989). Curriculum and evaluation standards for school mathematics. Reston, VA: Author.

Parker, W.C. (1991). Renewing the social studies curriculum. Alexandria, VA: Association for Supervision and Curriculum Development.

Perkins, P. (1993). Resource book for teachers. Orange, CA: Chapman University.

Perrone, V. (Ed.). (1991). Expanding student assessment. Alexandria, VA: Association for Supervision and Curriculum Development.

References *(cont.)*

Seely, A.E. (1994). <u>Discoveries and dilemmas: Views of assessment in three primary classrooms</u>. Unpublished manuscript.

Stenmark, J.K. (1991). <u>Mathematics assessment: Myths, models, good questions, and practical suggestions</u>. Reston, VA: National Council of Teachers of Mathematics.

Tierney, R.J., Carter, M.A., & Desai, L.E. (1991). <u>Portfolio assessment in the reading-writing classroom</u>. Norwood, MA: Christopher-Gordon Publishers.

Valencia, S.W. (1990a). Alternative assessment: Separating the wheat from the chaff. <u>The Reading Teacher, 44</u>, 60-61.

Valencia, S.W. (1990b). A portfolio approach to classroom reading assessment: The whys, whats, and hows. <u>The Reading Teacher, 43</u>, 338-340.

Valencia, S.W., Hiebert, E.H., & Afflerbach, P.P. (1994). <u>Authentic reading assessment: Practices and possibilities</u>. Newark, DE: International Reading Association.

Weaver, C. (1988). <u>Reading process and practice</u>. Portsmouth, NH: Heinemann.

Webb, N.L. (1993). Assessment for the Mathematics Classroom. In N.L. Webb & A.F. Coxford (Eds.), <u>Assessment in the mathematics classroom</u> (pp. 239-247). Reston, VA: National Council of Teachers of Mathematics.

Teacher Created Materials Reference List

TCM #773 Language Arts Assessment, Grades 1-2 (1994)
TCM #777 Language Arts Assessment, Grades 3-4 (1994)
TCM #781 Language Arts Assessment, Grades 5-6 (1994)

TCM #772 Social Studies Assessment, Grades 1-2 (1994)
TCM #776 Social Studies Assessment, Grades 3-4 (1994)
TCM #780 Social Studies Assessment, Grades 5-6 (1994)

TCM #771 Science Assessment, Grades 1-2 (1994)
TCM #775 Science Assessment, Grades 3-4 (1994)
TCM #779 Science Assessment, Grades 5-6 (1994)

TCM #770 Math Assessment, Grades 1-2 (1994)
TCM #774 Math Assessment, Grades 3-4 (1994)
TCM #778 Math Assessment, Grades 5-6 (1994)

TCM #506 Middle School Assessment (1994)